9-15

D1285201

ACROSTIC POEMS

BY LISA M. BOLT SIMONS

ILLUSTRATED BY KATHLEEN PETELINSEK

The Child's World

Published by The Child's World®
1980 Lookout Drive · Mankato, MN 56003-1705
800-599-READ · www.childsworld.com

ACKNOWLEDGMENTS
The Child's World®: Mary Berendes, Publishing Director
Red Line Editorial: Editorial direction
The Design Lab: Design and production

Photographs ©: Thinkstock, 7 (left); Fuse/Thinkstock, 7 (right); Jose Manuel Gelpi Diaz/Thinkstock, 13; Sebastian Crocker/Shutterstock Images, 18

ISBN 9781631436925
LCCN 2014945435

Printed in the United States of America
Mankato, MN
November, 2014
PA02240

About the Author

Lisa M. Bolt Simons is a writer and a teacher. She has published more than ten books for children. She has also been awarded grants and awards for her writing. Besides writing, teaching has been her passion for 20 years. She lives in Minnesota with her husband and boy/girl twin teenagers. Her Web site is *www.lisamboltsimons.com*.

About the Illustrator

Kathleen Petelinsek is a graphic designer and illustrator. She has been designing and illustrating books for children for 20 years. She lives in Minnesota with her husband, two dogs, a cat, and three fancy chickens.

TABLE OF CONTENTS

What Is a Poem?

Have you sung a song at a birthday party? Did you know you were singing a poem? Think about cards people buy for special occasions. Many cards have poems inside.

Poems are a special kind of writing. They have been around for thousands of years. Poems can be long or short. Some poems are only a few words. Others are as long as a book!

Several things make poems different from other kinds of writing. Most writing uses sentences. But poems use lines. A sentence has a complete thought. It also has punctuation. A line doesn't have to be a complete thought. Lines also don't need punctuation. Sometimes a whole poem has no punctuation!

Poets think very hard about the sounds the words in their poems make. Sometimes poets use words that **rhyme**. Rhyming words have the same ending sound. The words *flower* and *power* rhyme. So do *dog* and *frog*.

The word mouse *has one syllable.* Ze-bra *has two.*
Clap along as you say a word to hear the syllables.

All poems have **rhythm**. This is the pattern of sounds in a poem. The **syllables** in a line help decide a poem's rhythm. Syllables are the sounds that make up a word.

Some syllables are **stressed**. They are spoken more strongly. Other syllables are unstressed. They are spoken more softly. The word *HOUSE* has one stressed syllable. *BIRD-house* has two syllables. The first one is stressed.

Great
civilization
Really
good at
math and
science
EECE

WHAT IS AN ACROSTIC POEM?

Acrostics are one form of poetry. Poets pick a
special word when they write acrostics. Each letter
of the word begins a line of the poem. The lines of
the poem are about that word.

Acrostics have been around for thousands of
years. They were probably first written in ancient
Greece. People used them to share predictions about
future events.

Many poets pick a person's name for the titles of their acrostics. Each line describes the person. A line can be as short as one word!

Milk-drinker

Imaginative

Curly hair

Happy

Explorer

Left-handed

Learner

Eager

?

What is the name used in this acrostic?

Descriptive Acrostics

Acrostics are a great way to describe a person. But they can also describe a thing or an idea. Different parts of speech can be written for each letter. Nouns, verbs, and adjectives make up many of the words in an acrostic.

NOUNS, VERBS, AND ADJECTIVES

A noun is a person, place, or thing. *Boy*, *dinosaur*, and *Hawaii* are nouns. Verbs

say what a noun is doing. *Celebrates* and *tickles*
are verbs. An adjective is a word that describes
something. *Purple*, *scary*, and *big* are adjectives.
In an acrostic, poets often put nouns, verbs, and
adjectives together.

Nouns, verbs, and adjectives describe an acrostic's special word. Sometimes poets do this with just one word per line.

Spelling — NOUN
Chapters — NOUN
Homework — NOUN
Offers — VERB
Outstanding — ADJECTIVE
Learning — NOUN

The word that makes up an acrostic is usually not written as a word in the poem. *School* was not included in the poem you just read. The poet only uses words that help describe school.

Strong words and details create a better acrostic poem. Instead of saying something is "nice" or "gross," describe how it sounds or smells!

PHRASES

The "School" acrostic used one word per line. But many acrostic poems use several words in a line. Several words together make a phrase. Phrases are a combination of nouns, verbs, and adjectives. Phrases are parts of sentences. They let you describe something in detail.

Bask in the sun

Unique wing patterns

Travels near and far

Tickles your hand

Eggs into caterpillars
into cocoons

Rests at night

Flower nectar

Lepidoptera insects

Yellow and blue and
orange and green and
black and brown and white

What nouns are used in this poem?

15

CHAPTER THREE
3

Story Acrostics

Acrostic poems can also tell stories. All stories should have a beginning, middle, and end. Acrostic stories are usually very short and simple. Poets must choose their words carefully so readers know what is happening. In an acrostic about skateboards, the poet might tell the reader about a trick someone does on a skateboard. The words help the reader picture what's happening.

SETTING AND TONE

Setting is where a story takes place. This is not always spelled out in poems, but the reader may still be able to **infer** it. This means the reader can guess the setting based on the words the poet uses.

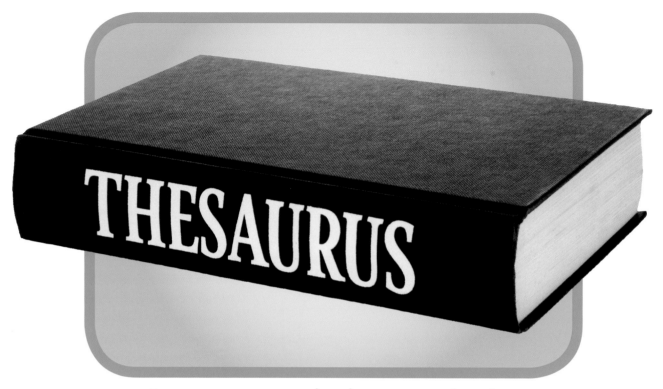

Poets try to use unusual and creative words in their acrostics. A thesaurus is a book that groups together words that mean similar things. A thesaurus can help you find creative words you might not think of!

The words in a poem often put pictures in readers' heads. These are called images. Poets create images in many different ways. They might use lots of adjectives. They might appeal to one of the five senses. Describing emotions also helps create images.

An acrostic that tells a story has **tone**. The tone of a poem is the emotion the writer wants to share with a reader. In a poem about spiders, one poet may write about how scared he is of a spider. He might use words like *squish* and *dreadful*. Another poet may have a pet spider that she loves. She might use words like *playful* and *extraordinary*.

Popped
Out
Pieces of
Corn in the palm
Of my hand
Ready to throw up in the air! . . . to hit my
Nose

?

What are the beginning, middle, and end of this story acrostic? Tell the story using regular sentences.

NOW IT'S YOUR TURN!

Writing acrostics can be a lot of fun.
You can write them about anything in the
world. All you need is a word to start with.
Now that you know more about acrostics,
it's time to write your own!

TIPS FOR YOUNG POETS

1. Start by writing acrostic poems using the name of someone you know. Use one-word adjectives. Then try writing phrases.

2. Think of your favorite animal. Then write an acrostic telling a story about it.

3. Incomplete thoughts are OK in poems. That means you don't always need to write words like *a* and *the*.

4. Ask a friend or family member to think of five words. Then write an acrostic for each word.

5. Learn how to write another kind of poem. Then write an acrostic and the new kind of poem on the same topic.

6. Make a list of interesting adjectives for each letter of the alphabet. Choose from these next time you write an acrostic.

7. Acrostic poems don't have to rhyme, but they can. See if you can write an acrostic that rhymes.

8. Read as many poems as you can. Reading poems makes you a better poet.

GLOSSARY

appeal (uh-PEEL): To appeal is to suggest or encourage something. Poets often appeal to the five sense in acrostic poems.

infer (in-FUR): To infer is to use facts and details to make a good guess about something. When you read an acrostic, you infer the poem's meaning.

rhyme (RIME): Words that rhyme have the same ending sound. The words *cake* and *snake* rhyme.

rhythm (RITH-uhm): Rhythm is a repeating pattern of sounds in poetry. Music also has a rhythm.

stressed (STREST): A word is stressed when it is said a bit stronger or louder than another word or syllable. The pattern of stressed and unstressed words decides a poem's rhythm.

syllables (SIL-uh-buhlz): Syllables are units of sounds in a word. You can tell how many syllables are in a word by clapping your hands as you say the word.

tone (TOHN): Tone is the attitude or emotion felt by a writer toward a subject. An acrostic can have a hopeful tone or a sad tone.

TO LEARN MORE

BOOKS

Hardley, Avix. *African Acrostics: A Word in Edgewise.* Somerville, MA: Candlewick Press, 2012.

Minden, Cecilia, and Kate Roth. *How to Write a Poem.* North Mankato, MN: Cherry Lake Publishing, 2011.

Prelutsky, Jack. *Pizza, Pigs, and Poetry: How to Write a Poem.* New York: Greenwillow Books, 2008.

ON THE WEB

Visit our Web site for lots of links about acrostics: www.childsworld.com/links

Note to Parents, Teachers, and Librarians: We routinely check our Web links to make sure they're safe, active sites—so encourage your readers to check them out!

INDEX